Cambridge **Discovery Education**™

▶ **INTERACTIVE READERS**

Series editor: Bob Hastings

JEFF CORWIN
WILD MAN

A1

Kenna Bourke

 **CAMBRIDGE** UNIVERSITY PRESS

 **Discovery** EDUCATION™

CAMBRIDGE UNIVERSITY PRESS
Cambridge, New York, Melbourne, Madrid, Cape Town,
Singapore, São Paulo, Delhi, Mexico City

Cambridge University Press
32 Avenue of the Americas, New York, NY 10013-2473, USA

www.cambridge.org
Information on this title: www.cambridge.org/9781107680395

First published 2014

Printed in Hong Kong, China, by Golden Cup Printing Company Limited

A catalog record for this publication is available from the British Library.

Library of Congress Cataloging-in-Publication Data

Bourke, Kenna.
  Jeff Corwin : wild man / Kenna Bourke.
    pages cm. -- (Cambridge discovery interactive readers))
  ISBN 978-1-107-68039-5 (pbk. : alk. paper)
  1. Corwin, Jeff--Juvenile literature. 2. Biologists--United States--Biography--Juvenile literature.
  3. English language--Textbooks for foreign speakers. 4. Readers (Elementary) I. Title.

QL31.C73B68 2013
570.92--dc23
[B]

                          2013025111

ISBN 978-1-107-68039-5

Additional resources for this publication at www.cambridge.org

Layout services, art direction, book design, and photo research: Q2ABillSMITH GROUP
Editorial services: Hyphen S.A.
Audio production: CityVox, New York
Video production: Q2ABillSMITH GROUP

Contents

Before You Read: Get Ready! 4

CHAPTER 1
"The Things I Do for You Guys!" 6

CHAPTER 2
The Early Years 8

CHAPTER 3
The Jeff Corwin Brand 12

CHAPTER 4
The Life of a Wild Man 16

CHAPTER 5
What Do You Think? 20

After You Read 22

Answer Key 24

Glossary

Before You Read:
Get Ready!

Some people say it's important to study and learn about animals. But why are animals important, and who is interested in them?

Words to Know

Look at the pictures. Then complete the sentences below with the correct words.

bugs

elephant

ocean

snake

TV show

1 _____ are small animals with six legs – some of them can fly.

2 An _____ is a big body of salty water.

3 A _____ is something you watch at home, sometimes every week.

4 This long animal with no legs is a _____ .

5 An _____ is a big animal. It lives in Africa or India.

Words to Know

Read the paragraph. Then complete the sentences below with the correct highlighted words.

Animals are often scared of people. Why? It's because sometimes we do bad things to animals. We can hurt them. Because we hurt them, some species of animals, like tigers, are dying. A naturalist is a person who studies living things, like animals. Naturalists usually want to protect animals so they don't get hurt and die.

1. Ouch! I _____ my hand.

2. Young children often get _____ at night.

3. People want to _____ small animals and babies.

4. Cats and dogs are different _____. A cat and a dog can't make babies together.

5. Jeff Corwin is a _____. He knows a lot about animals because he studies them.

A crocodile

CHAPTER 1

"The Things I Do for You Guys!"

WHO IS THIS MAN?

He flies in planes, swims in oceans, sleeps outside, and walks across deserts.[1] He travels to many countries, writes books, and is on TV. He loves animals, eats **strange** things, gets hurt sometimes, and he . . . RUNS! Often he runs very fast. Why? Usually because an animal is behind him!

But who is he?

Meet Jeff Corwin. Many people know about him because they see him on TV. He has an important job, but a difficult one. Jeff is a naturalist. He knows a lot about animals from all over the world, and he teaches people about them.

[1]**desert:** a very hot place with not many plants and little water

Jeff travels to lots of places. Sometimes, he helps people study animals. Jeff went to Australia to study bats. Bats live in big groups. In the day they sleep in caves. They wake up at night. That's when you can see them.

Sometimes bats **bite** people. That's bad news because some bats have diseases.[2] People can get their diseases, so it's important to know what diseases the bats have.

Bats sleep in caves.

It's difficult to study bats. They don't like people very much, and they get scared when people come near them. But that doesn't stop Jeff!

....
[2]**disease:** something that makes people or animals feel very bad or sick

Video Quest

Big Bats

Watch the video of Jeff Corwin catching bats. Why does Jeff need to see a doctor?

An aquarium

CHAPTER 2

The Early Years

**DO WE LIKE SNAKES IN OUR HOUSES?
NO, NOT REALLY!**

It's 1973, and Jeff is six years old. He's playing outside at his grandparents' house. He sees a snake for the first time. He doesn't know it's a snake. The snake is big. It's almost as big as Jeff!

He picks it up and it bites him. Then he goes into the house with the snake. Jeff's grandmother says, "Get that out of the house!" She doesn't want a big snake in her house!

Jeff doesn't understand. He says, "No!"

His grandmother asks, "Why?"

Jeff answers, "Because I love it!"

A frog

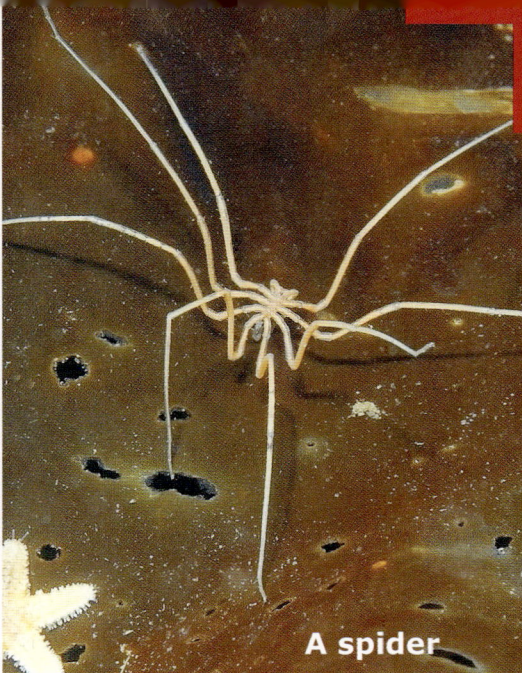

A spider

That's a true story. It's how Jeff's love of animals began. **Even** today, Jeff is very interested in snakes.

Jeff says that he was never scared of animals, not even as a very young child. Jeff and his family lived near Boston, a city in the United States. Jeff made his bedroom into a small zoo!

He found bugs, spiders, snakes, and frogs and put them in aquariums. Sometimes he put water animals in the toilet. Jeff's parents' friends were scared to use the bathroom!

For Jeff, these animals weren't pets. He studied them, and then he put them back in their homes outside.

At age 13, Jeff wanted to see more snakes. He wanted to study snakes in Belize, a country in Central America, but his parents said no. They didn't want to go with him and they thought Jeff was too young to travel **alone**.

Jeff also needed money to travel to Belize. So he started working after school and on weekends. He worked in restaurants and put the money away for his **trip**.

Finally, at age 16, he went to Belize. He went to the rainforest and studied many animals. He was happy because he saw a lot of snakes!

In college,[3] Jeff studied animals. He was very interested in bats and snakes.

[3]**college:** a place where you study after you finish high school

The rainforest in Belize

Video Quest

For the Love of Snakes

Watch the video to see Jeff pulling a snake from the water. Who is helping him?

Jeff filming a show for Animal Planet with a rescued seal.

For some time, Jeff thought he wanted to be a teacher in college. Next, he thought he wanted to study more about animals. But then he had a better idea.

In 1994, Jeff was in Belize again. He went there to work with his friend, Bob Ballard, on *The Jason Project*. This project helps students learn more about science. One day, Bob showed some of Jeff's work on TV and that was it! Jeff found his "dream job."

He wanted to teach people, but not at college – on TV!

CHAPTER 3

The Jeff Corwin Brand

YOU CAN LEARN AND HAVE FUN AT THE SAME TIME.

Jeff thinks a good **way** to teach people is to entertain[4] them. People learn better when they're having fun. And Jeff likes to have fun!

On his TV shows, Jeff says funny things about the animals, birds, and fish he finds. That's one of the **reasons** why Jeff Corwin is a TV star. He started making shows in 1997, and now he makes TV shows for ten months every year.

Jeff is famous at home in the United States and in many countries in the world. Jeff says, "It's pretty cool when you're in a far off land and someone knows you."

[4]**entertain:** keep people interested

A great white shark

?

EVALUATE

Is it always fun to be a TV star like Jeff? Why or why not?

Jeff's first TV show, with the Disney Channel, was *Going Wild with Jeff Corwin*. Next, he started working with Animal Planet and the Discovery Channel to make *The Jeff Corwin Experience* and *Corwin's Quest*. It was these shows that really made him famous. Animal Planet is on TV in more than 80 countries!

On these shows, you can see Jeff meeting a great white shark. Or you can watch him having a bad time playing with an elephant. The elephant on the show hurts Jeff's arm a lot. But is Jeff scared? No, he isn't.

A coconut tree

This is one of the biggest species of clam.

Animal shows aren't the only shows Jeff does. In 2003, Jeff was in *CSI: Miami*, a police show. What did he do? He helped the police take someone's foot out of a crocodile's mouth, of course!

In 2009, Jeff was on *Extreme Cuisine*, a show about cooking around the world. On that show, Jeff climbs tall trees to get coconuts. He also eats some geoducks – one of the world's biggest clams.

Because Jeff is famous, people often ask him to be on their shows, too. Oprah Winfrey talked to him on her show, and you can see him on TV news shows. The president of Colombia even asked Jeff to visit his family.

Jeff has more than 60,000 friends on Facebook. That's a lot! Why is Jeff so **popular**? It's because he's funny and also because he's not often scared – even when animals want him for dinner!

But there's another very important reason. Jeff Corwin is a conservationist. He does a lot of work to protect animals. Because people sometimes do things that are bad for animals, some animals don't have places to live or food to eat. Many animals die because of people. Did you know that a species of animal dies every 20 minutes?

Jeff works hard to protect animals and to teach people to be good to them.

A wasp

CHAPTER 4

The Life of a Wild Man

A DAY IN JEFF CORWIN'S LIFE IS NEVER BORING. TAKE A LOOK!

Hungry? Eat a bug!

Jeff travels around the world. He eats some strange things. On the food show *Extreme Cuisine*, Jeff goes to Mexico. There, he works with an old man from a small village. They look for *chiricoco*, a kind of bug that you can eat. In Southeast Asia, Jeff finds people catching a type of wasp you can eat.

He learns a lot about the way people live. On his TV shows, he tells us that many people in the world eat things like bugs. It is an easy way to get food that is good for you.

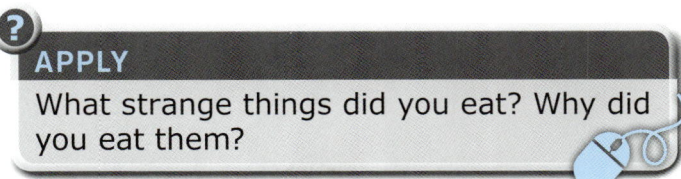

?

APPLY

What strange things did you eat? Why did you eat them?

Maybe you don't eat bugs, but why not? Maybe they're good to eat. And maybe they're good for you!

The snakebite!

Jeff has a tattoo[5] of a snake on his left arm, and it isn't only because he likes snakes. When Jeff was a young man, he worked a lot in Belize. One day, he was alone in the rainforest, and a coral snake bit him. Coral snakes can **kill** people with one bite.

Jeff didn't die. He got to the doctor in time. But his wife, Natasha, wasn't very happy with him! "You can't do that!" she said. "You have a family now." Maybe Jeff's tattoo tells him to watch out!

....

[5]**tattoo:** a kind of picture

A coral snake

A peregrine falcon

As fast as a bird?

In *Corwin's Quest*, Jeff tries to do some things animals can do. In one show, Jeff studies the peregrine falcon. This bird can fly very fast. It can fly at 320 kilometers an hour. It's faster than any other animal in the world.

But Jeff does more than watch the falcon. He asks questions, too. How does the falcon feel? Is it fun to fly at 320 kilometers an hour?

To find the answers, Jeff jumps off a **bridge** at the same time as the falcon flies. He jumped from the bridge ten times to get the answers to his questions!

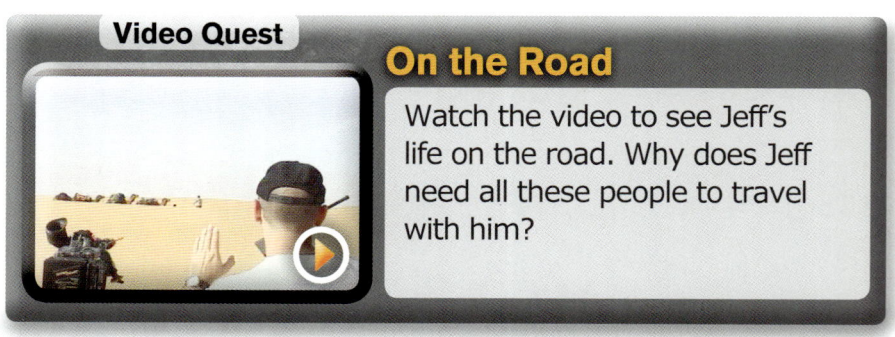

Video Quest

On the Road

Watch the video to see Jeff's life on the road. Why does Jeff need all these people to travel with him?

Back home

Sometimes, but not very often, Jeff doesn't work. But Jeff doesn't like to get on a plane and go on a vacation. He likes to stay at home with his wife and his two daughters.

So where does Jeff live and what does he do there? Well, he lives on an island[6] near Boston. In his house there are many strange things. For example, Jeff has a lot of masks – about 60! He brought them back from different countries.

The Corwins think a lot about the food they eat. They catch fish from the ocean to eat. And they have their own fruit trees.

There are cats in the back yard. And of course, there are a few snakes, too!

....

[6]**island:** land that has water all around it

Masks

Swimming with a shark

CHAPTER 5

What Do You Think?

JEFF CORWIN SAYS THAT SOMETIMES PEOPLE AND ANIMALS AREN'T VERY DIFFERENT.

One day Jeff was with some baby elephants. The babies didn't have parents because some people killed them. Many of the babies died, too, but nobody knew why.

Jeff found that baby elephants like to sleep next to something warm. So one night, Jeff slept next to a baby elephant. That night the elephant was warm and happy. It played with Jeff's hair. Jeff's daughter did the same thing when she was a baby!

So maybe Jeff is right. People and animals often need the same things.

Jeff Corwin's love of animals started at a very young age. He now has his dream job and is famous for it. Life is good!

In his TV shows, he does some strange things and some fun things, but he sometimes gets hurt. A snake bit him. An elephant hurt his arm!

Look at the list of things Jeff does. Do they scare you? Which would you like to try? Why?

- swim with sharks
- jump off a bridge to see how fast a bird flies
- catch a snake
- study bats
- eat and cook bugs in Mexico
- make a TV show about animals

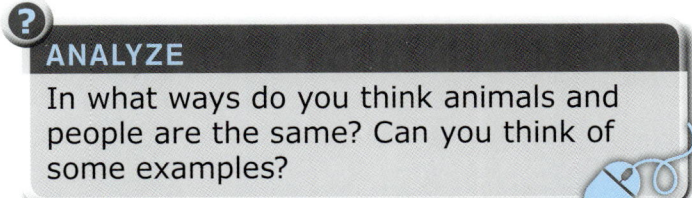

?

ANALYZE

In what ways do you think animals and people are the same? Can you think of some examples?

After You Read

Read the sentences and choose Ⓐ, Ⓑ, or Ⓒ.

1 Jeff Corwin saw his first snake _____.
- Ⓐ in the rainforest of Belize
- Ⓑ at his grandparents' house
- Ⓒ on an island near Boston

2 Jeff thinks a good way to teach people is by _____.
- Ⓐ having fun
- Ⓑ swimming
- Ⓒ cooking food

3 When Jeff was 16, he went to _____.
- Ⓐ college
- Ⓑ Belize
- Ⓒ Australia

4 Jeff does animal shows. He also did _____.
- Ⓐ doctors' shows
- Ⓑ weather shows
- Ⓒ cooking shows

5 Jeff is a naturalist. He's also a _____.
- Ⓐ conservationist
- Ⓑ policeman
- Ⓒ zookeeper

6 Jeff teaches people how to _____.
- Ⓐ eat strange things
- Ⓑ fly planes
- Ⓒ help animals

7 The tattoo on Jeff's arm helps him remember _____.
- Ⓐ to call his wife and daughters
- Ⓑ to watch out for snakes
- Ⓒ not to play with elephants

8 Sometimes Jeff isn't working. Then he likes to _____ .

    Ⓐ stay at home

    Ⓑ go to Australia

    Ⓒ catch bats

My Opinion

Write down three things Jeff does. Why do you think these things are important?

What Jeff does	Why it is important
1.	
2.	
3.	

Complete the Sentences

Use the words in the box to complete the sentences.

bugs	hurt	ocean	protect	species

1 Watch out! The snake is going to _____ you!

2 I like the _____ because I can swim in it.

3 The mother elephant wants to _____ her baby.

4 There are many _____ of birds in the world.

5 Jeff sometimes eats _____ .

Answer Key

Words to Know, page 4
❶ Bugs ❷ ocean ❸ TV show ❹ snake ❺ elephant

Words to Know, page 5
❶ hurt ❷ scared ❸ protect ❹ species ❺ naturalist

Video Quest, page 7
He needed to see a doctor because a bat bit him. Bats can give people a disease.

Video Quest, page 10
Maria and the guys help him.

Evaluate, page 13
Answers will vary.

Apply, page 17
Answers will vary.

Video Quest, page 18
It's difficult to make a TV show. You need a lot of people to do different things.

Analyze, page 21
Answers will vary.

Choose the Correct Answers, page 22
❶ B ❷ A ❸ B ❹ C ❺ A ❻ C ❼ B ❽ A

My Opinion, page 23
Answers will vary.

Complete the Sentences, page 23
❶ hurt ❷ ocean ❸ protect ❹ species ❺ bugs